Illustrator:
Barb Lorseyedi

Editor:
Janet Cain, M. Ed.

Editorial Project Manager:
Ina Massler Levin, M.A.

Editor in Chief:
Sharon Coan, M.S. Ed.

Art Director:
Elayne Roberts

Cover Artist:
Larry Bauer

Production Manager:
Phil Garcia

Imaging:
David Bennett
Hillary Merriman

Publishers:
Rachelle Cracchiolo, M.S. Ed.
Mary Dupuy Smith, M.S. Ed.

T5-CCV-648

September
Monthly Activities

Early Childhood

Author:
Dona Herweck Rice

Teacher Created Materials, Inc.
P.O. Box 1040
Huntington Beach, CA 92647
©1996 Teacher Created Materials, Inc.
Made in U.S.A.
ISBN-1-55734-860-X

Table of Contents

Introduction

The monthly activity books in this series have been created specifically for early childhood students. Every book is divided into four themes, approximately one theme per week of the month. Within each weekly theme, there is a lesson sheet; a parent sign in/out sheet; a list of suggested home activities; a number of thematic activities, such as arts and crafts, stories, letters, numbers, colors, shapes, music, movement, and food; a just-for-fun page; an original poem; stationery; clip art and patterns; bookmarks and badges for rewards; and an award certificate for one area of achievement. A calendar pattern, to which each child can add dates and a picture, and a request letter are included for the entire month. The themes for the month of September are *school, Grandparents' Day, apples,* and *farms.* A variety of management materials have been included to support each theme, creating a unifying whole.

All activities are designed to enhance motor and/or cognitive skills while students are having fun. Most importantly, the activities have been classroom tested—with excellent results.

Use some or all of the pages to support the already exciting early childhood experiences taking place in your classroom.

September Calendar

Sunday	Monday	Tuesday	Wednesday	Thursday	Friday	Saturday

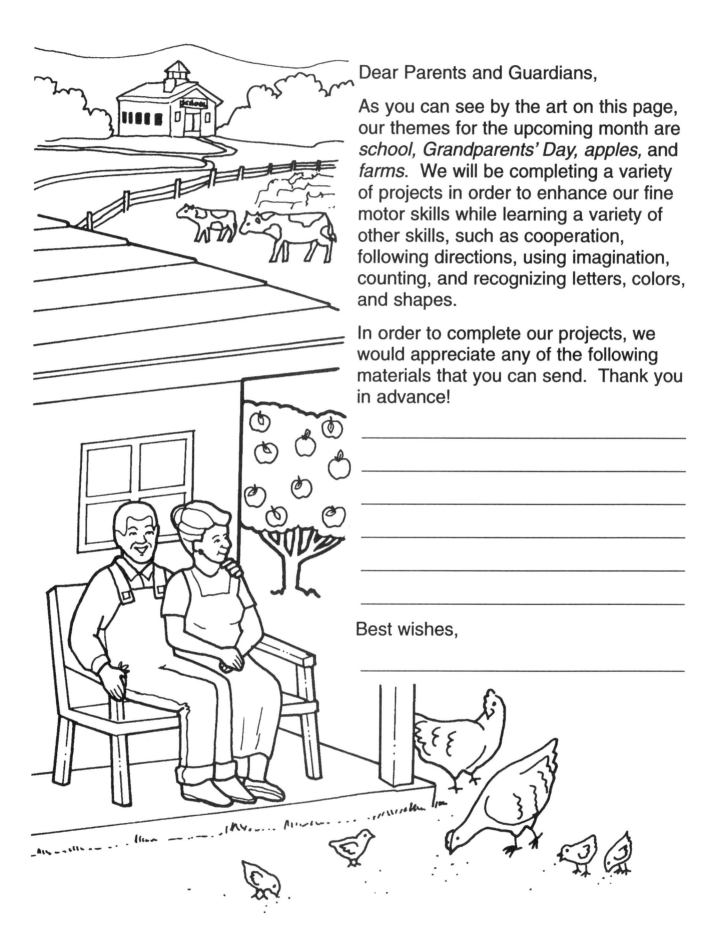

Dear Parents and Guardians,

As you can see by the art on this page, our themes for the upcoming month are *school, Grandparents' Day, apples,* and *farms.* We will be completing a variety of projects in order to enhance our fine motor skills while learning a variety of other skills, such as cooperation, following directions, using imagination, counting, and recognizing letters, colors, and shapes.

In order to complete our projects, we would appreciate any of the following materials that you can send. Thank you in advance!

_____

_____

_____

_____

_____

Best wishes,

_____

Activity (circle time, playtime, etc.)	Monday	Tuesday	Wednesday	Thursday	Friday

Parent Sign In/Out Sheet

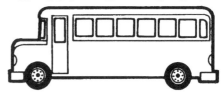

Parents: Please sign your child in and out under the current date.

Name	Time	Date:	Date:	Date:	Date:	Date:
	In					
	Out					
	In					
	Out					
	In					
	Out					
	In					
	Out					
	In					
	Out					
	In					
	Out					
	In					
	Out					
	In					
	Out					
	In					
	Out					
	In					
	Out					

School Activities for Home

Dear Parents and Guardians,

Our theme of the week is *school*. Below is a list of enjoyable activities that you can do with your child. Please use some or all of these activities to support your child's learning. Your help is greatly appreciated.

Suggested Activities:

- Play school together. Let your child be the teacher. Provide paper, crayons, pencils, glue, scissors, and, if possible, a small chalkboard, chalk, and eraser.

- Take your child to a local library. Help your child check out a school storybook or nonfiction book. Read it together. Discuss your favorite parts with one another.

- Each of you can draw and color a picture of yourself at school. Tell about your pictures.

- Tell your child a story about a school experience you had. Show school or yearbook photographs of yourself if you have them.

- Together, watch a video for children that shows school as a prominent setting. Suggested videos include *Madeline* (Heron Communications, Inc., 1989), *Barney's Making New Friends* (The Lyons Group, 1995), and *Barney's All Aboard for Sharing* (The Lyons Group, 1996). Each of you can discuss what you see and how you feel. Act out your favorite parts of the movie.

- Include casual conversations about school while doing other activities, such as driving in the car, sitting at the dinner table, and eating breakfast.

- Read "Big Kid School" with your child. If your child does not yet attend an elementary school, ask what he or she imagines big kid school will be like. If your child already attends an elementary school, ask what he or she imagines school is like for an older student.

Best wishes,

_____

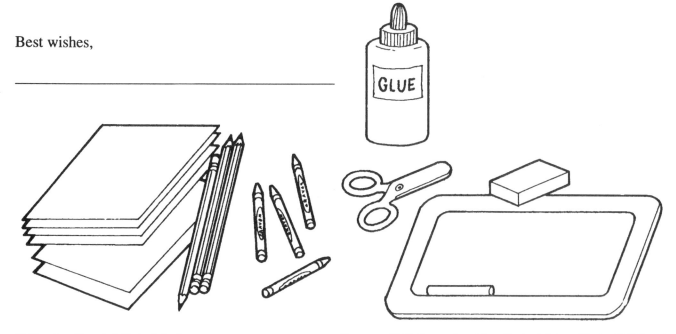

School Arts and Crafts

Materials:

- square pattern (below, one per student)
- schoolhouse pattern (page 9 copied onto red paper, one per student)
- scissors and crayons

Directions:

1. Let each student cut out the patterns, or you can cut them out ahead of time. Have students cut the schoolhouse doors along the dotted lines and fold them open.

2. Students should draw pictures on the square patterns to show how they feel or how they think they will feel about attending elementary school. Then each student can dictate or write a sentence to describe the feeling. You may wish to write the dictated sentence on scrap paper and have the student copy it onto the square pattern.

3. Squeeze glue onto each square pattern around the edges and paste it behind the doors of the schoolhouse pattern so the picture can be seen when the doors are opened.

Alternative: You can change the sentence stems on the patterns so they are relative to your lessons. For example, if students are learning about the letter **A**, change the sentence stem on the schoolhouse pattern to "I can read the letter _____." Delete the sentence stem on the square pattern and have students write and color a giant **A**.

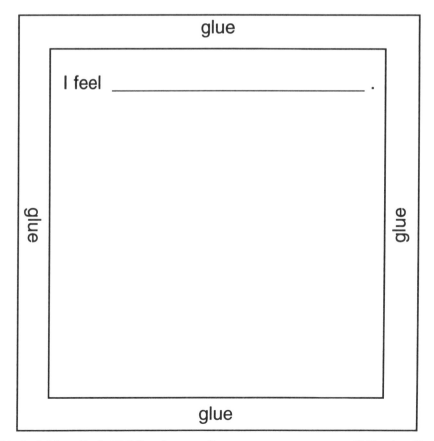

School Arts and Crafts *(cont.)*

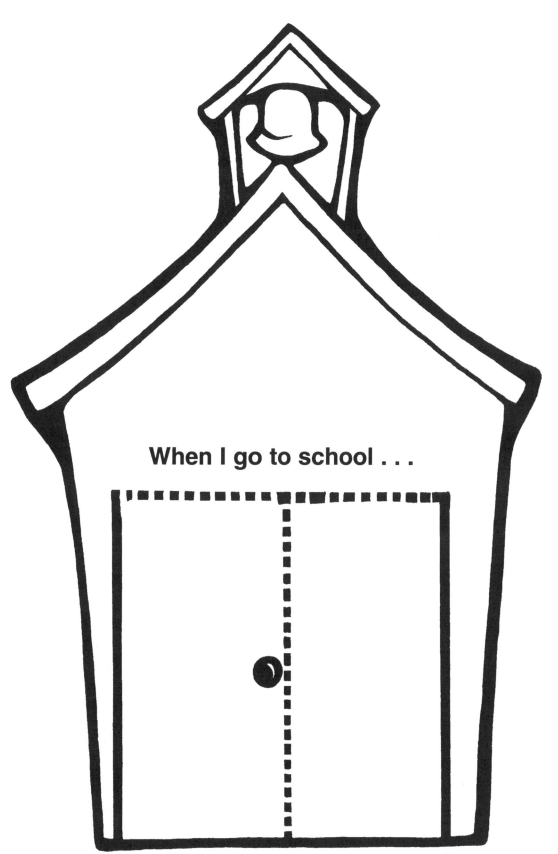

When I go to school . . .

School Story

Talk with the students about school and the kinds of things that happen there. Write their ideas on the chalkboard or butcher paper, marking each student's name next to the statements he or she makes. Then give each student the pattern shown below. Write one of his or her ideas on the lines and let the student illustrate it. Create a class book by collecting all the pages and stapling them or punching holes and tying them together with yarn. Read the entire book to the class.

School Letters

Students can practice matching their uppercase and lowercase letters with the project provided below and on the next page. Duplicate both pages onto heavy paper. Cut out the letter strips, tape the two upper-case strips together, and then tape the two lowercase strips together. Cut out the slate. Then use a craft knife to cut the slate along the dotted lines. Be sure that students do not handle the knife. Color the slate as desired or let each student color his or her own. Thread the uppercase strip through the top opening so that one letter at a time shows. Thread the lowercase strip through the bottom opening in the same way. Let students practice matching their upper- and lowercase letters by sliding the strips until the correct match appears.

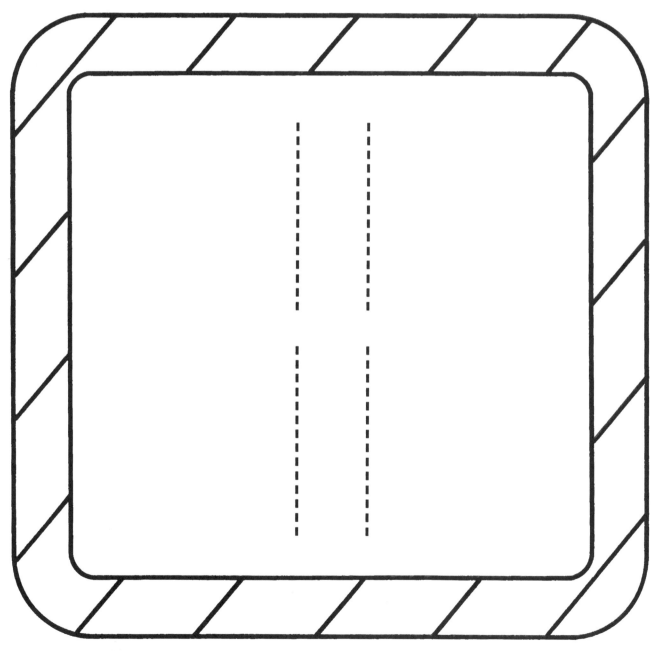

A reward badge for this activity can be found on page 22.

School Letters *(cont.)*

L M W Q P F J N V H E U G

C K B D R Y T I O A S X Z

l q h b g p a s u j w i f

o c v e y k r m x n z d t

School Numbers

Draw lines matching each number to the bus with that many children.

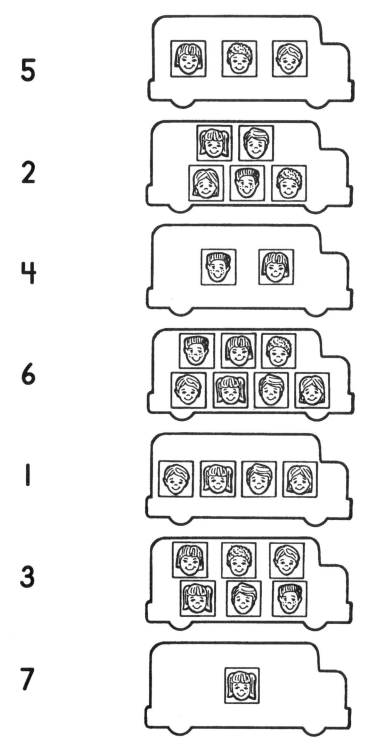

5

2

4

6

1

3

7

Note: Make a large school bus to hang on your classroom wall by enlarging the pattern on page 20. Laminate it. Each day, place a different number of faces in the bus windows. Have students count them as part of the morning routine.

School Colors

When we think of school buildings, we often think of the color red. Use a red crayon or pencil to color everything on this page that is also often red.

rose	moon
cow	cherries
window	apple
bricks	baseball

A reward badge for this activity can be found on page 22.

School Shapes

Trace the shapes shown below onto sponges and cut them out. Pour tempera paint onto a Styrofoam tray or plate. You may wish to provide different colors of paint. Provide students with white construction paper. Let them make sponge paintings by dipping one side of each sponge into the paint and then stamping the paper with the sponges. Invite students to make as many prints as they like.

Note: Inform parents ahead of time of the date for this project since it will be a messy day. You can send notes to parents on the school stationery (page 19), asking them to send old shirts or smocks if you do not already have some.

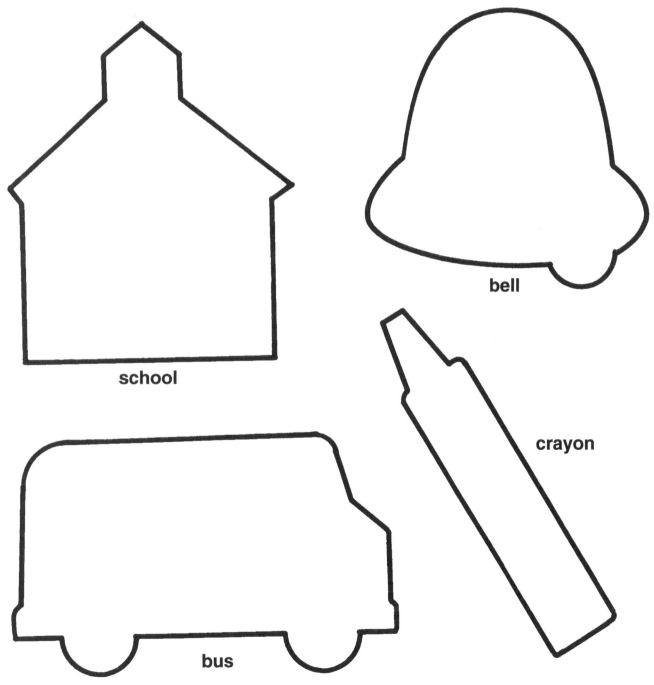

school

bell

crayon

bus

School Food

While learning about schools, students can make and enjoy some tasty alphabet pretzels. This recipe yields approximately 16 pretzels. Mix two batches to make the entire alphabet.

Note: Ask parents if their children have any food allergies or dietary restrictions.

Ingredients:

- 1 package active dry yeast
- 1 teaspoon (5 mL) table salt
- 1 egg, beaten
- $3\frac{1}{2}$ to 4 cups (875 mL to 1 L) all-purpose flour (if flour is self-rising, omit salt)
- $1\frac{1}{2}$ cups (375 mL) warm water
- 1 teaspoon (5 mL) sugar
- coarse salt

Materials:

- 2 large mixing bowls
- measuring cups and spoons
- electric beaters
- clean dish towel
- small mixing bowl
- mixing spoon
- cutting board
- cooking oil
- spatula
- pastry brush
- cookie sheets
- oven

Preparation:

1. Use a large mixing bowl to dissolve the yeast in warm water.
2. Stir in the table salt, sugar, and half the flour. Beat until smooth.
3. Stir in enough of the remaining flour to make the dough easily manageable.
4. Knead the dough on a lightly floured cutting board until smooth and elastic (about 5 minutes).
5. Place the dough in a greased bowl. Then rotate the dough so that the greased side is facing up. Cover the bowl with a clean dish towel and let the dough rise until it doubles in size (about 45–60 minutes). The dough is ready if it does not spring back when touched.
6. Heat the oven to 425° F (220° C).
7. Punch the dough down and cut it into 16 equal parts. Roll each part into a thin rope about 12–18" (30–45 cm) long.
8. Give each student a dough rope with which to form a letter. You may wish to have students make the first letters of their first names or designate specific letters in order to create the entire alphabet.

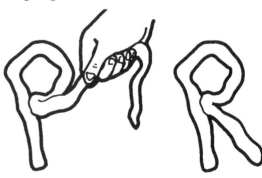

9. Place the letters on greased cookie sheets, brush them with beaten egg, and sprinkle coarse salt on them.
10. Bake the pretzels until they are brown (about 15–20 minutes) and cool them on a wire rack.
11. A reward badge for this activity can be found on page 22.

Alternative: Buy frozen bread dough. Thaw it and let students shape letters, as described above. Bake as directed, shortening the time required due to the small size of the letters.

School Maze

Help the children get to school on time.

Big Kid School

Sometimes I see the big kid school,
And I can tell it's really cool.

I know they do all kinds of things,
Like ride their bikes and play on swings.

Maybe they learn to build a car.
I bet they even play guitar.

I wonder if they paint the walls
And run some races down the halls.

I'll bet they know all kinds of stuff
But never seem to learn enough.

They sing some songs, they act in plays,
They read and write and draw all day.

They learn to whistle and to snap
And how to dance ballet and tap.

They fly some kites and do some flips
And build some model sailing ships.

Gee, I bet it will be so cool
When I go to the big kid school!

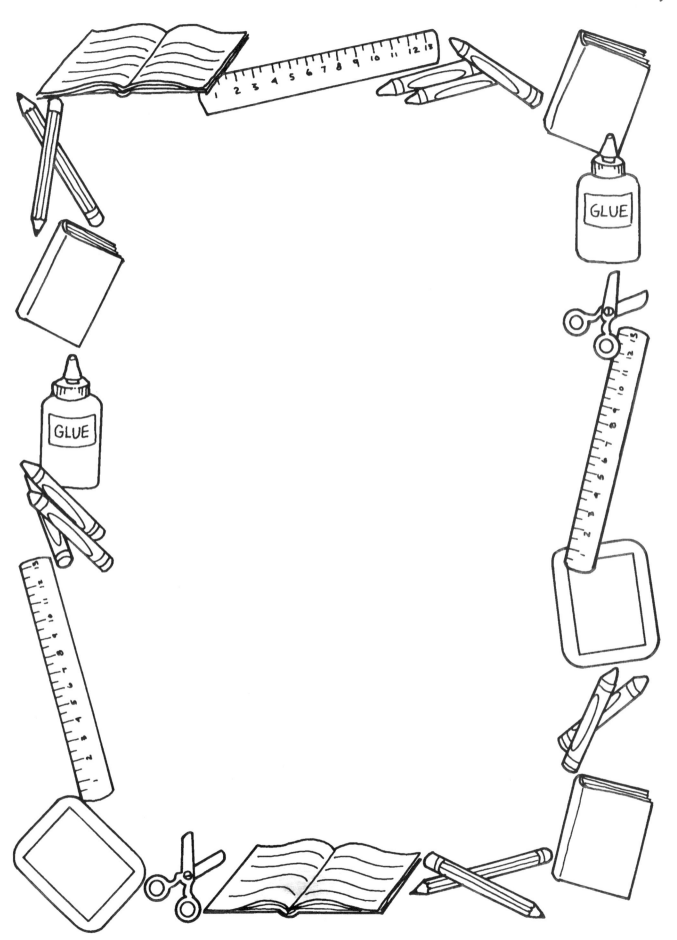

Clip Art and Patterns

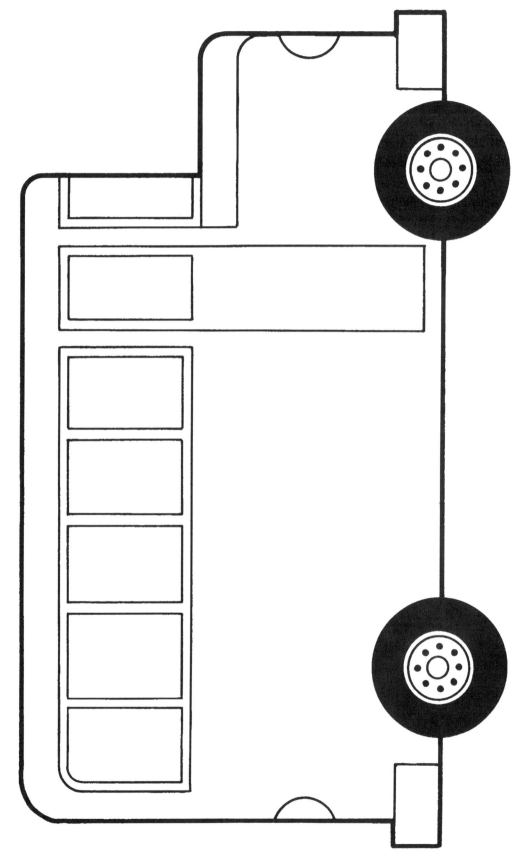

Clip Art and Patterns *(cont.)*

Bookmarks and Badges

I know the
color red.

Have students color the crayon red and
wear the badge home.

I can
match uppercase
and lowercase letters.

AaBbCcDdEeFfGgHhIi
JjKkLlMmNnOoPpQqRr
SsTtUuVvWwXxYyZz

Have students color their
badges and wear them home.

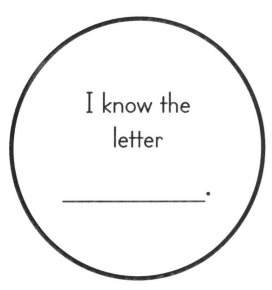

I know the
letter

_____.

Have each student write in the pretzel
letter he or she made. Students can
color their badges and wear them home.

Although most early childhood students
have not yet learned to read, they enjoy
having bookmarks to use while reading
with their families at home.

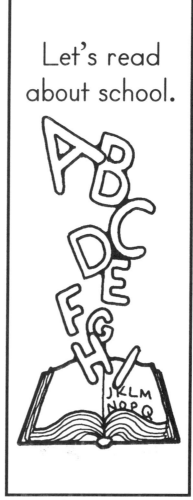

Let's read
about school.

School
is cool.

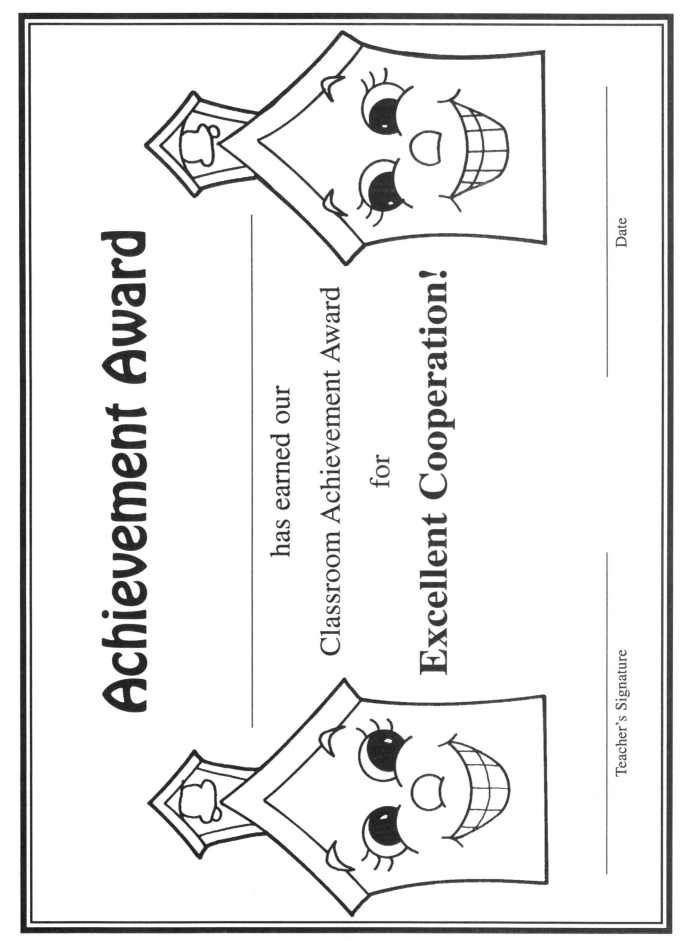

Achievement Award

has earned our

Classroom Achievement Award

for

Excellent Cooperation!

Date

Teacher's Signature

Activity (circle time, playtime, etc.)	Monday	Tuesday	Wednesday	Thursday	Friday

Parent Sign In/Out Sheet

Parents: Please sign your child in and out under the current date.

Name	Time	Date:	Date:	Date:	Date:	Date:
	In					
	Out					
	In					
	Out					
	In					
	Out					
	In					
	Out					
	In					
	Out					
	In					
	Out					
	In					
	Out					
	In					
	Out					
	In					
	Out					
	In					
	Out					

Grandparents' Day Activities for Home

Our theme of the week is *Grandparents' Day*. Below is a list of enjoyable activities that you can do with your child. Please use some or all of these activities to support your child's learning. Your help is greatly appreciated.

Suggested Activities:

- If your child has grandparents, allow him or her to give them a call or visit. Encourage the grandparents to share some stories about themselves. If your child does not have grandparents, you might consider "adopting" an older adult friend as an honorary grandparent. This relationship is an important one to a child.

- Ask your child what makes a person a grandparent and what are some special things about grandparents. Then read "What Makes a Grandparent?" together and discuss it.

- Provide your child with materials to make greeting cards for his or her grandparents or older adult friends in honor of Grandparents' Day, which is celebrated the second Sunday in September.

- Take your child to a local library. Help your child check out a storybook or nonfiction book about grandparents. Read it together. Discuss your favorite parts with one another.

- Each of you can draw and color a picture of grandparents and grandchildren. Tell about your pictures.

- If they are available, look through old family photographs of your child's grandparents and other ancestors. Explain the family relationships to him or her.

- Look at a world map with your child. Show where your ancestors came from.

- Help your child make a family tree. Tell your child about something special you once did with one or more of your grandparents.

- Ask your child about his or her favorite grandparent memories.

- Together, list all the things you can that have to do with grandparents.

Best wishes,

_____

Grandparents' Day
Arts and Crafts I

Here is a whole-class project in celebration of Grandparents' Day.

Materials:

- large poster board
- old magazines
- scissors
- glue

Directions:

1. Enlarge the letter **G** shown below on the poster board. Tell students that this is a **G** for *grandparents*.

2. Let students look through the magazines, tearing out pictures of grandparents or things that remind them of grandparents.

3. Trim the pictures. If they are able, let students do this.

4. Create a collage by gluing the pictures onto the letter **G**.

Alternative: Reproduce the letter **G** shown above enlarging it to fill a whole page. Allow students to make individual collages as gifts for their grandparents.

Grandparents' Day
Arts and Crafts II

Reproduce the card shown below onto heavy paper. Have students color and decorate their cards as gifts for their grandparents or for people living in a nearby retirement or nursing home. If you are planning to take students with you to deliver the cards to the retirement or nursing home, be sure to call ahead of time to arrange the visit. You may wish to have students present a song, poem, or skit.

Grandparents' Day Story

Together with the class, read Mercer Mayer's two books entitled *Just Grandma and Me* (Golden Press, 1983) and *Just Grandpa and Me* (Golden Press, 1985). Both are Little Critter stories.

Afterwards, give each student a copy of the bottom portion of this page. Ask students to choose whether they would like to draw their grandmas or grandpas. Let them write an *m* or *p* on the line depending on whom they would like to draw. Then ask them to draw pictures showing themselves with their grandparents. (**Note:** If a student does not have a grandparent, you can change the wording on the page to either "Just Mom and Me," "Just Dad and Me," or another appropriate substitute.) Collect all of the pages, add a cover page with any title the class would like, and staple the pages together to make a class book.

Just Grand _____a and Me

Grandparents' Day Letters

Practice the letter **G** for grandparents. Have students color in the giant letters on this page. Then ask them to write a row of uppercase **G**'s and a row of lowercase **g**'s across the bottom of the page.

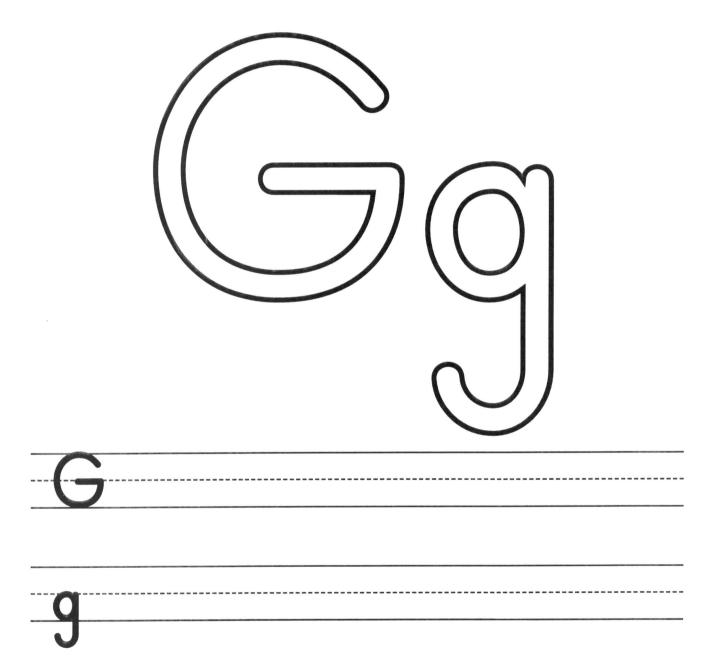

A reward badge for this activity can be found on page 41.

Grandparents' Day Numbers

Ask students how old they are. Have them show you with their fingers. Then ask them how old they think grandparents are. Explain to them that grandparents can be many ages, but generally the youngest grandparents may be around forty and the oldest may be more than one hundred.

Let students experience these higher numbers by asking each of seven parents to bring in sets of small objects. Tell parents that the objects can be returned to them. Each set should consist of the same type of object. The sets should be in increments of ten, ranging from 40 to 100. Object suggestions include uncooked macaroni, beads, buttons, paper clips, marbles, dry beans, popcorn kernels, pennies, and feathers.

Put each set of objects in a clear plastic container. Let students look at them and estimate how many they think are in each jar. After they have estimated, label each jar with the exact number. In small groups, let them take one set of objects out of the jar, sort them into smaller groups, and put them back together again.

To complete this activity, as a class choose a number between 40 and 100. Go outdoors on a leaf, twig, or pebble collecting expedition. Be sure to take a bag or other container. Have students collect the leaves, twigs, or pebbles until you have gathered the number they have chosen.

Grandparents' Day Colors

Though many of us grew up believing that grandparents had gray or white hair, we know this is often not really the case. Ask each student to think about the hair color of one of his or her grandparents or older adult friends/relatives. Since young children sometimes have difficulty remembering such details, you may wish to use the stationery on page 38 to send a note home asking for this information ahead of time. Explain to parents that the purpose of this activity is to learn about colors and not to pry. Use the following activity after students have selected hair colors.

Materials:

- head pattern (page 33, precut; one per student)
- construction paper or yarn (variety of colors, including gray, white, black, dark brown, light brown, red, blue, orange, and yellow)
- scissors
- glue
- crayons

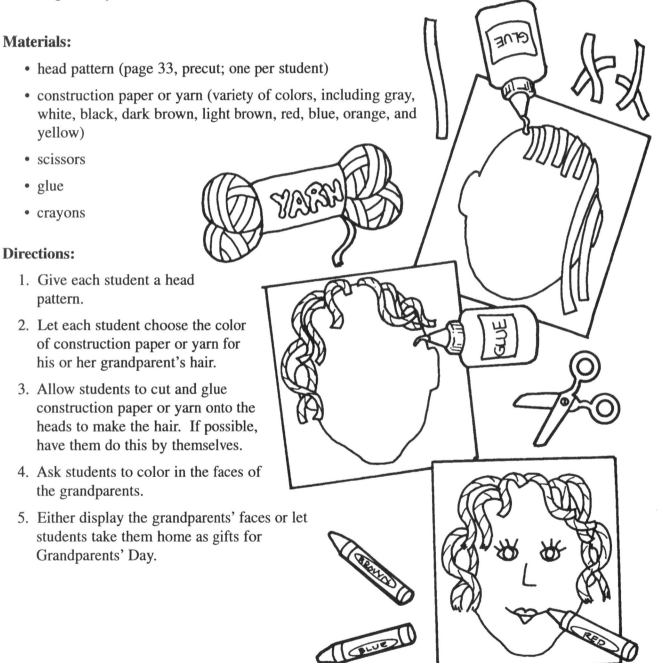

Directions:

1. Give each student a head pattern.

2. Let each student choose the color of construction paper or yarn for his or her grandparent's hair.

3. Allow students to cut and glue construction paper or yarn onto the heads to make the hair. If possible, have them do this by themselves.

4. Ask students to color in the faces of the grandparents.

5. Either display the grandparents' faces or let students take them home as gifts for Grandparents' Day.

A reward badge for this activity can be found on page 41.

Grandparents' Day Colors *(cont.)*

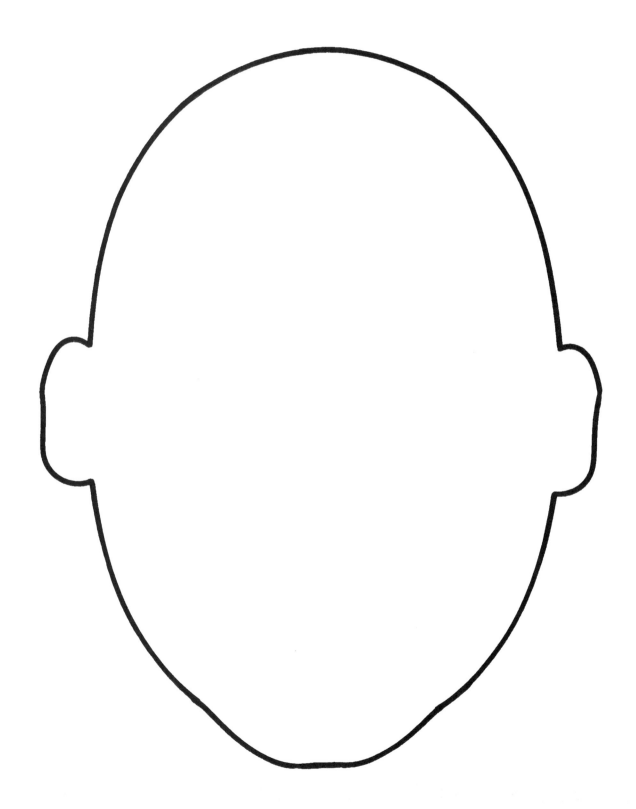

Grandparents' Day Music

There are many songs for today's children that have been popular since their grandparents were young. Perhaps some of the songs your students know were taught to them by their grandparents.

To bring this musical history into your classroom, send home the note that is provided below. Prepare for a day of music, fun, and intergenerational sharing. To top it all off, serve delicious homemade cookies (page 35) just like the kind Grandma or Grandpa might make.

Dear Parents,

In celebration of Grandparents' Day, we are inviting the grandparents of our students to come into our classroom for a small party on _____ at _____.
Date   *Time*

We would like the grandparents to share with the class some of their favorite songs from childhood, preferably those songs that may still be familiar to the children today. We will have a sing along, serve some treats, and get all the benefits of spending time with our grandparents. Our grandparents will, of course, get the benefit of spending time with some super grandchildren.

If your child's grandparents are available and would like to come, please fill out the form below and return it by _____ .
Date

Thank you,

_____

Yes, _____'s grandmother/grandfather can attend the party on
Child's Name

_____ at _____.
Date   *Time*

He/she will share the song _____.
Song Title

He/she can be reached at _____ .
Phone Number

_____
Parent Signature

Grandparents' Day Food

Here is a wonderful recipe for some old-fashioned cookies just like Grandma or Grandpa might make. The recipe yields approximately five dozen oatmeal-raisin or oatmeal-chocolate chip cookies.

Note: Ask parents if their children have any food allergies or dietary restrictions.

Ingredients:

- ¾ cup (190 mL) shortening
- ½ cup (125 mL) granulated sugar
- ¼ cup (65 mL) water
- 1 teaspoon (5 mL) salt
- 1 teaspoon (5 mL) cinnamon
- ½ teaspoon (3 mL) cloves
- 1 cup (250 mL) all-purpose flour (if self-rising, omit salt and baking soda)

- 1 cup (250 mL) brown sugar, packed
- 1 egg
- 1 teaspoon (5 mL) vanilla
- 3 cups (750 mL) quick-cooking oats
- ½ teaspoon (3 mL) baking soda
- 2 cups (500 mL) raisins or chocolate chips

Materials:

- oven
- hot pads
- mixing bowl
- measuring cups
- shortening or non-stick cooking spray

- cookie sheets
- spatula
- large spoon
- measuring spoons
- reclosable storage container

Preparation:

1. Heat the oven to 350° F (180° C).

2. Combine the shortening, brown sugar, granulated sugar, egg, water, and vanilla in a bowl and mix thoroughly.

3. Use the large spoon to stir in the remaining ingredients.

4. Grease the cookie sheets with shortening or non-stick cooking spray.

5. Drop round teaspoonfuls of dough onto the cookie sheets about 2" (5 cm) apart.

6. Bake for 12–15 minutes or until there is almost no imprint remaining after you touch the cookies with your finger. Immediately remove the cookies from the sheets when they are done.

7. To keep the cookies fresh, place torn pieces of white bread among the cookies and store them in a tightly covered container.

Names for Grandmother and Grandfather

Around the world, grandparents are called by many different names. As a class, brainstorm to list some of the names given to grandmothers and grandfathers. Ask students to include what they call their grandparents.

Grandmother   **Grandfather**

_____   _____

_____   _____

_____   _____

_____   _____

_____   _____

_____   _____

A reward badge for this activity can be found on page 41.

What Makes a Grandparent?

What makes a grandparent?
It's easy to tell.
But it's not glasses
Or a cookie smell.

It's not a garden
Or silvery hair.
It's not fishing poles
Or a rocking chair.

What makes a grandparent?
You probably know.
Loving a grandchild
Is what makes them so.

Clip Art and Patterns

Note: Let students fill in their own details of what a grandmother and a grandfather look like.

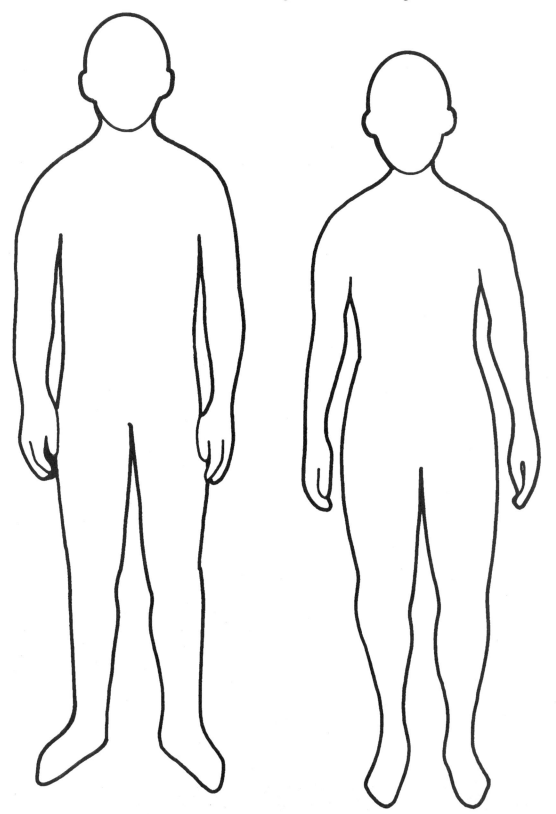

Clip Art and Patterns *(cont.)*

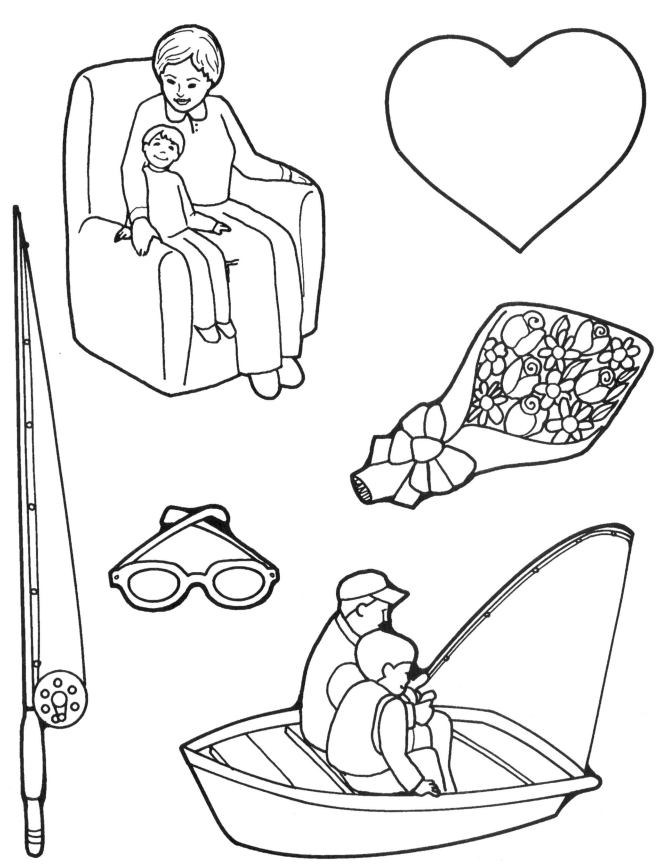

Bookmarks and Badges

_____ is my name for grand___a.

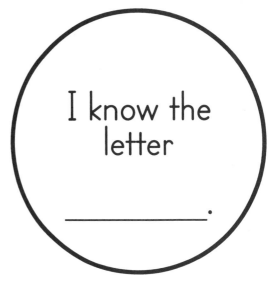

I know the letter _____.

Write in each student's name for either grandmother or grandfather. Let students color their badges and wear them home.

Have students color their badges and wear them home.

I know the color _____.

Let each student dictate the color of the hair he or she has used on page 32. Have students color their badges and wear them home.

Although most early childhood students have not yet learned to read, they enjoy having bookmarks to use while reading with their families at home.

Let's read about grandparents.

Grandparents mean love.

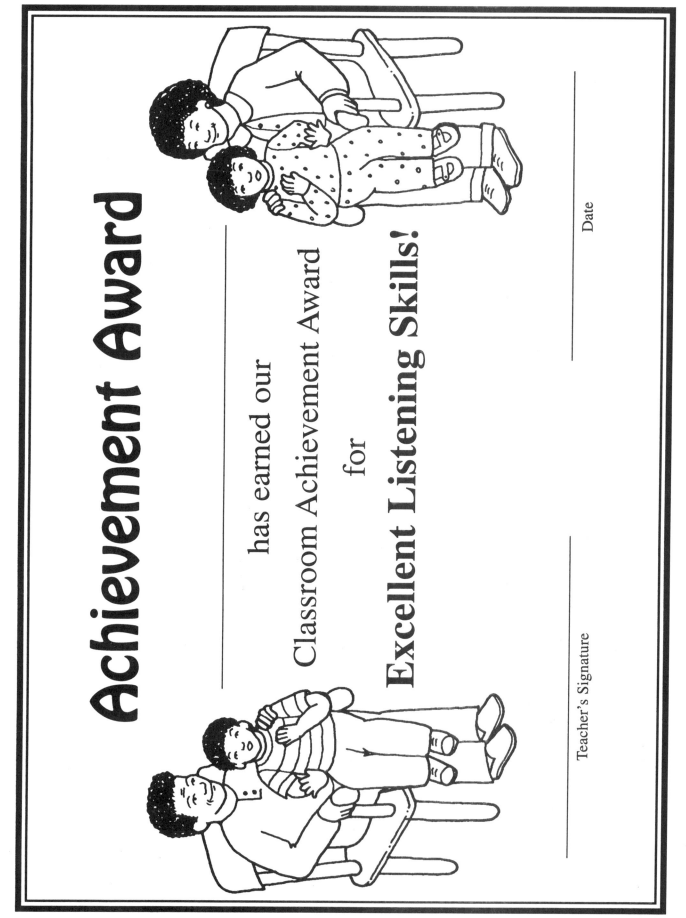

Achievement Award

has earned our

Classroom Achievement Award

for

Excellent Listening Skills!

_____
Date

_____
Teacher's Signature

Activity (circle time, playtime, etc.)	Monday	Tuesday	Wednesday	Thursday	Friday

Parent Sign In/Out Sheet

Parents: Please sign your child in and out under the current date.

Name	Time	Date:	Date:	Date:	Date:	Date:
	In					
	Out					
	In					
	Out					
	In					
	Out					
	In					
	Out					
	In					
	Out					
	In					
	Out					
	In					
	Out					
	In					
	Out					
	In					
	Out					
	In					
	Out					

Apple Activities for Home

This week we will be learning about *apples*. Below is a list of enjoyable activities that you can do with your child. Please use some or all of these activities to support your child's learning. Your help is greatly appreciated.

Suggested Activities:

- Enjoy some apples, applesauce, apple juice, and other foods made from apples.

- Visit an apple orchard. Talk with your child about what the two of you see there.

- When at the market, look at the different kinds of apples there. Ask your child to name their colors.

- Take your child to a local library. Help your child check out a storybook or nonfiction book about apples. Read it together. Discuss your favorite parts with one another.

- Imagine together that you are apple trees. What do you and your child imagine an apple tree might say, think, or do? Also imagine you are apples on the tree. Pantomime growing on the tree and then falling to the ground or being picked.

- Each of you can draw and color a picture of an apple or an apple tree. Tell about your pictures.

- Cut an apple open with your child. Ask your child what he or she sees inside. Notice the pattern of the seeds.

- Wear clothes that are the colors of apples.

- Read and/or talk about Johnny Appleseed. You may also wish to watch the video entitled *Johnny Appleseed* (Prism Entertainment Corp., 1972).

- Find some pictures of apple blossoms and explain to your child how apples grow from the blossoms.

- Read "Eating Apples" with your child. Practice saying the poem together with lots of expression. Afterwards, pantomime eating apples.

Best wishes,

_____

Apple Arts and Crafts

Read any storybook about Johnny Appleseed, such as the one by Steven Kellogg (Morrow, 1988). Discuss with the class what you read. Then do the project below.

Materials:

- skillet hat patterns (page 47)
- pencil
- stapler
- gray construction paper
- scissors
- crayons

Directions:

1. Ahead of time, trace the hat patterns onto gray construction paper. Prepare one set per student. Either cut them out yourself, invite a parent volunteer to do it, or let students cut out their own.

2. Give each student a set of pattern pieces. Staple the handle to the skillet.

3. Tell students to place their skillets upside down on their desks or tables. You may need to model this for them. While the skillets are upside down, have each student color a picture of apples, apple trees, apple blossoms, or Johnny Appleseed.

4. Cut gray construction paper bands that are approximately 16" (40 cm) long and 2" (5 cm) wide, one per student.

5. Staple the ends of each band onto the back bottom corners of a skillet pattern, making sure that it fits the head of the student.

6. A reward badge for this activity can be found on page 60.

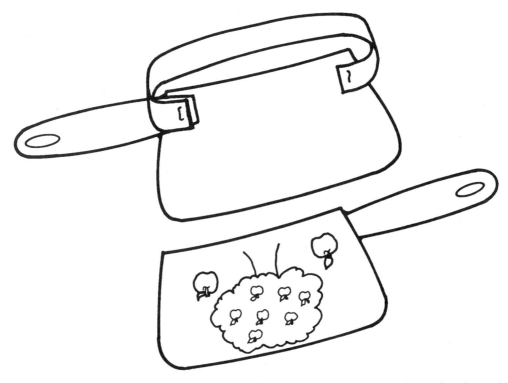

Apple Arts and Crafts *(cont.)*

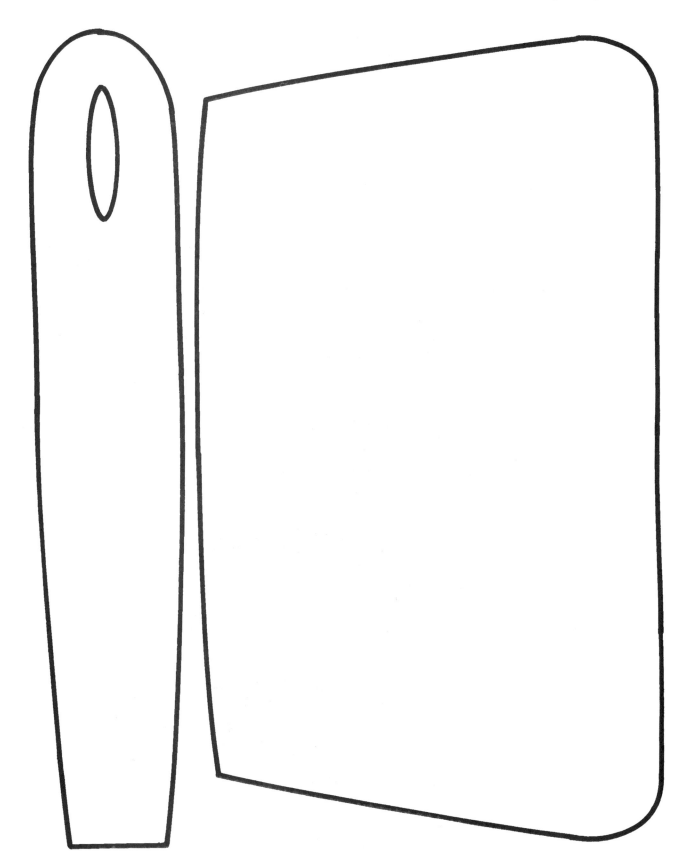

Apple Story

Follow the directions shown below for a novel approach to a class book. You will make a large apple tree, and students will illustrate apples to hang on it. Their apples will be the pages of the book.

Materials:

- brown paper bags
- scissors
- stapler
- pencil

- green construction paper or butcher paper
- apple pattern (page 49), reproduced on white paper
- tape
- crayons

Directions:

1. Cut the brown paper bags to form a tree trunk. For a more realistic, three-dimensional look, crumple and twist the bags. Staple them in a tree trunk shape onto a large bulletin board or tape them onto the classroom door or a section of wall.

2. Cut the green paper to form the leaves of the tree. Do not cut the leaves separately but, rather, cut them as one large mass for the entire top of the tree. Staple or tape the leaves to the top of the trunk.

3. Give each student a copy of the apple pattern. You may wish to cut out these patterns ahead of time or let each student cut out a pattern.

4. Read aloud the sentence stem on the pattern. Invite each student to dictate a way to complete the sentence as you write it on the pattern. Then let students color their apples.

5. Use tape to affix the apples to the tree, and read the book to the class.

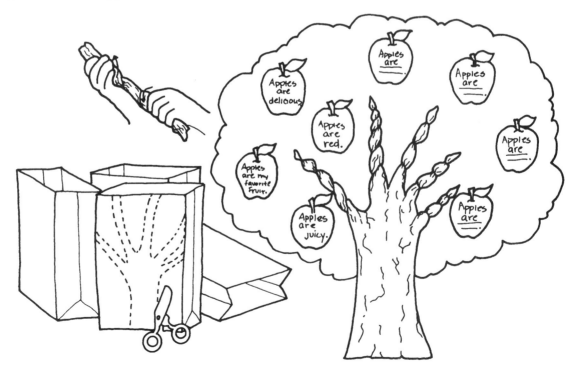

Apple Story (cont.)

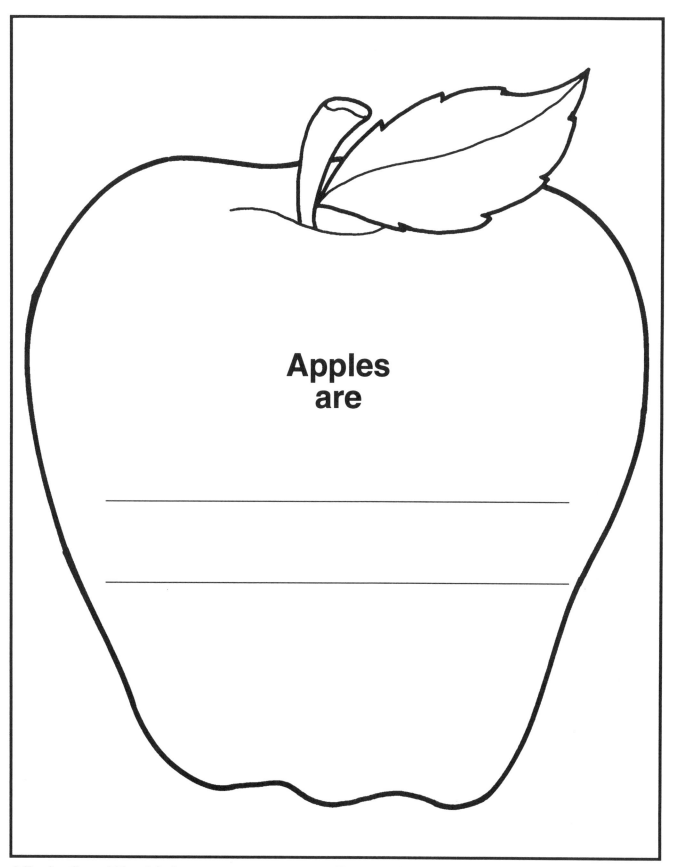

**Apples
are**

Apple Letters

Practice the letter **A** for *apples*. Have students color the giant letters on this page. Then have them color the apples.

A reward badge for this activity can be found on page 60.

Apple Colors

Materials:

- yellow, red, and green tempera paints
- sponges, cut into approximately 2" (5 cm) squares or circles
- apple pattern (page 58, one per student)
- sturdy paper plates
- scissors
- old shirts or smocks (one per student)

Directions:

1. Inform parents ahead of time of the date for this project since it will be a messy day. You can send notes to parents on the apple stationery (page 57), asking them to send old shirts or smocks if you do not already have some.

2. Give each student a copy of the apple pattern on page 58 and a smock to cover their clothes. **Note:** Do not cut out the apple patterns ahead of time.

3. Pour yellow, red, and green paint into separate paper plates. Place several sponges with each plate.

4. Let each student choose a color of paint. Then have students use the sponges to pat the paint onto their apples. Tell students to dip and pat the sponges as many times as necessary to cover the apples with paint.

5. Let the paint dry.

6. When they are dry, either trim around the apples yourself or let students do it. Hang your apples for display.

7. Give each student a color badge (page 60) as a reward. Have each color the apple on the badge the same color he or she painted the apple in this project.

Apple Shapes

Use the following directions to have each student make an apple tree, using circles and a rectangle.

Materials:

- green, red, and brown construction paper
- patterns (below)
- white or light blue construction paper
- scissors
- glue

Directions:

1. Prepare for this activity by using the patterns shown below to cut the following shapes for each student: one large green circle, five small red circles, and one brown rectangle.

2. Give each student a set of shapes and model the construction of an apple tree. Let students glue their pieces down on the white or light blue construction paper.

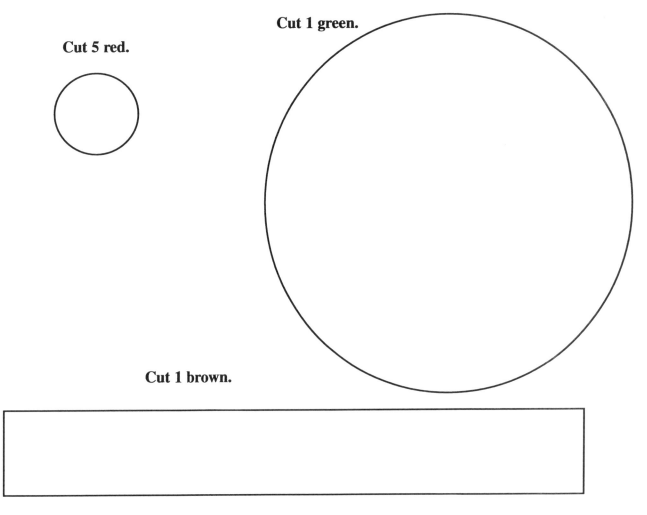

Cut 5 red.

Cut 1 green.

Cut 1 brown.

Apple Food

Apples are not only healthful but delicious, too. Try tasting different kinds of apples with students and charting their responses. Bring in, or ask parent volunteers to bring in, four or five kinds of apples. Cut them into small slices so that students can taste each type of apple. Write the name of each type of apple in the column on the left and color the picture to show what color each apple is.

Now have students taste the same type of apple. Ask students to raise their hands if they like that type of apple. Tape a red circle or affix an apple sticker for every student who likes that kind of apple. Then try the next type of apple. Continue in this manner until all of the apples have been tasted. Have students count the total number of votes for each kind of apple and record that information in the column on the right. Ask them to examine the chart to decide which kind of apple the class likes best.

Kinds of Apples	How Many Like This Type of Apple?	Total

Apple Food *(cont.)*

Apple pie is many people's favorite apple food. Here is a delicious recipe for apple crisp, a variation on apple pie. Make it in the classroom or send the recipe home with students to make with their parents. This recipe yields one apple crisp.

Note: If making the recipe in the classroom, have parent volunteers pare and cut the apples ahead of time. Students should not handle the knife. In addition, be sure to ask parents if their children have any food allergies or dietary restrictions.

Ingredients:

- 1 tablespoon (15 mL) water
- 1 tablespoon (15 mL) sugar
- ¼ teaspoon (1.25 mL) cinnamon
- 1 medium-sized cooking apple (i.e., Granny Smith)
- 1½ tablespoons (25 mL) all-purpose flour
- 1 tablespoon (15 mL) butter, softened

Materials:

- oven
- 10-ounce (300 g) custard cup
- hot pads
- paring knife
- small mixing bowl
- fork

Preparation:

1. Heat the oven to 350° F (180° C).

2. Pare and slice the apple to fill about 1 cup (250 mL).

3. Place the sliced apple into the custard cup.

4. Sprinkle the water over the apple.

5. Place the remaining ingredients in the mixing bowl. Blend together with a fork until they are crumbly.

6. Sprinkle the mixture over the apple.

7. Bake uncovered for 25–30 minutes or until the apple is soft and the topping is golden brown.

An Apple a Day

Who is saying hello to you from this delicious apple? Follow the dots to find out. Then color the picture.

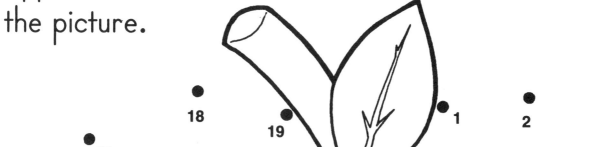

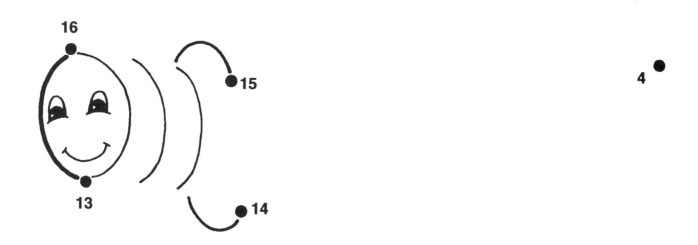

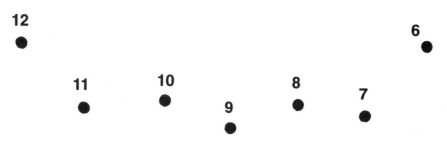

Eating Apples

Some are crunchy and some are so sweet.
Apples are such a delicious treat.

Eat them at mealtime or for a snack.
Take one along in your school backpack.

Green apples, red apples, yellow ones, too—
I like all these apples. How about you?

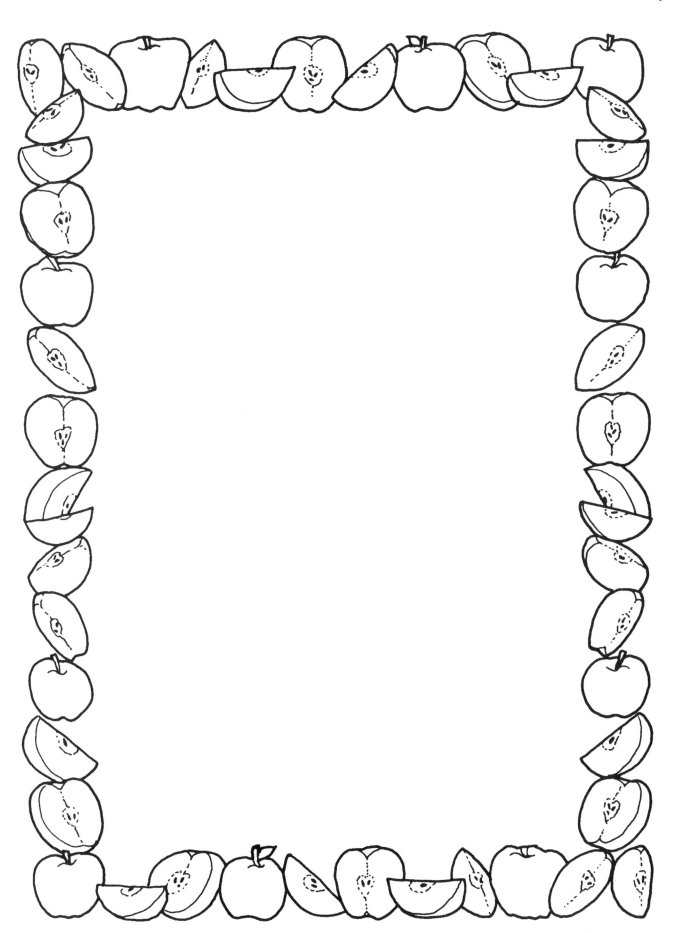

Clip Art and Patterns

Clip Art and Patterns *(cont.)*

Bookmarks and Badges

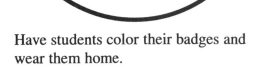

Have students color their badges and wear them home.

Have each student color the apple the same color (red, yellow, green) he or she painted the apple on page 51. Let them wear the badges home.

Although most early childhood students have not yet learned to read, they enjoy having bookmarks to use while reading with their families at home.

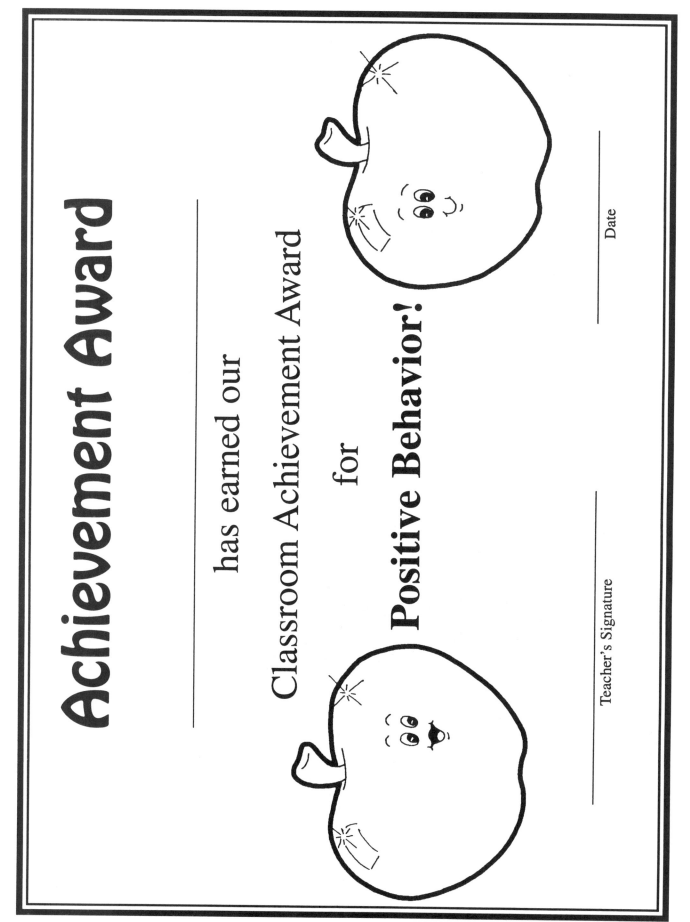

Achievement Award

has earned our

Classroom Achievement Award

for

Positive Behavior!

_____
Teacher's Signature

_____
Date

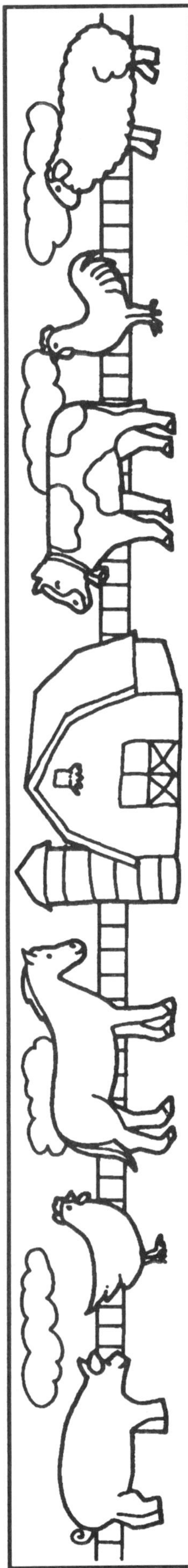

Farms

                                                                                            Lesson-Planning Sheet

Activity (circle time, playtime, etc.)	Monday	Tuesday	Wednesday	Thursday	Friday			

#860 September Monthly Activities—Early Childhood   62   © *Teacher Created Materials, Inc.*

Parent Sign In/Out Sheet

Parents: Please sign your child in and out under the current date.

Name	Time	Date:	Date:	Date:	Date:	Date:
	In					
	Out					
	In					
	Out					
	In					
	Out					
	In					
	Out					
	In					
	Out					
	In					
	Out					
	In					
	Out					
	In					
	Out					
	In					
	Out					
	In					
	Out					

Farm Activities for Home

This week we will be learning about *farms*. Below is a list of enjoyable activities that you can do with your child. Please use some or all of these activities to support your child's learning. Your help is greatly appreciated.

Suggested Activities:

- Brainstorm with your child to name different animals that live on a farm. Ask your child to make the sound each animal makes. Together, pantomime being each of these animals.

- Take your child to a local library. Help your child check out a farm storybook or nonfiction book. Read it together. Discuss your favorite parts with one another.

- Each of you can draw and color a picture of a farm or a farm animal. Tell about your pictures.

- If you ever lived or visited on a farm, tell your child about it.

- If you live on a farm now, ask your child what his or her favorite things about the farm are.

- Visit a nearby farm, fair, petting zoo, or anyplace where your child can see farm animals up close.

- Together, watch the video *Charlotte's Web* (Paramount Home Video, 1972). Discuss the differences between fantasy and reality. Cite examples from the video for each.

- Read "Old MacTavish" with your child. Talk about the strange things seen on Old MacTavish's farm. Ask what else your child thinks might be seen there.

- Together sing children's songs that are about farms or farm animals. Examples include "Old MacDonald," "Bingo," and "Baa, Baa, Black Sheep."

- With your child, compare and contrast life on a farm with life in a city.

Best wishes,

_____

Farm Arts and Crafts I

A variety of farm animals, such as a pig, cow, sheep, and goat, can be made from the pattern shown below and on page 66. Copy the patterns onto appropriately colored construction paper.

Invite students to draw on details such as facial features, feet, and hair. Students can also glue on spots and an udder for a cow, cotton balls for the wool of a sheep, and a cotton goatee for a goat. They will need to add appropriate tails, as shown below.

Place on a fold.

Farm Arts and Crafts I *(cont.)*

Farm Arts and Crafts II

Reproduce the patterns shown below and on page 67 for students. Let students color and cut out their own set of patterns. Help them put the patterns together by placing paper fasteners at the X's, as shown. While swinging the horse's legs, students can recite the following rhyme:

Trotting, trotting through the day,
Galloping, galloping down the way.
Neigh to the left, neigh to the right,
Running, running out of sight.

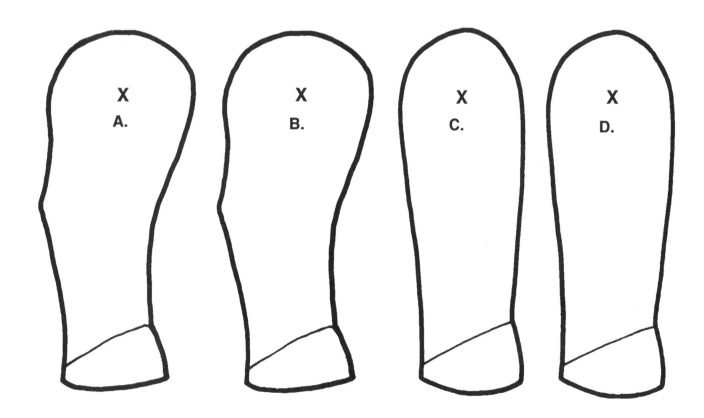

X
A.

X
B.

X
C.

X
D.

Farm Arts and Crafts II *(cont.)*

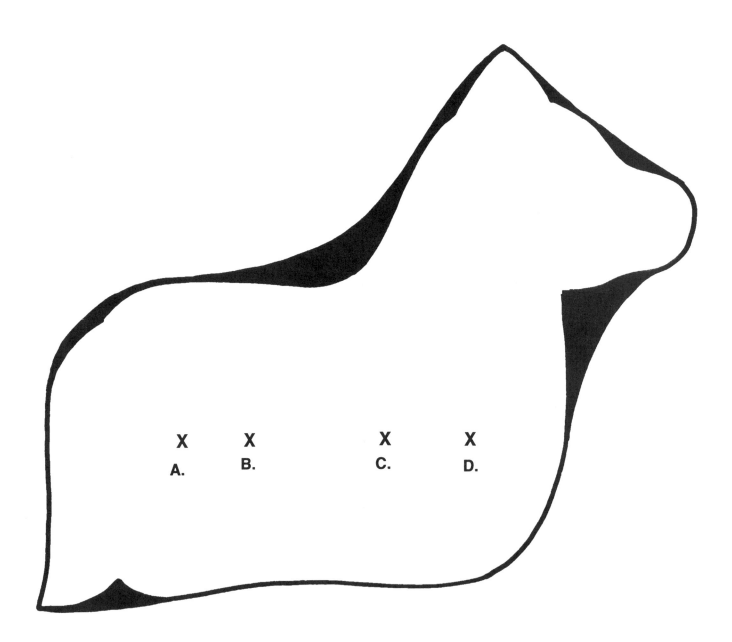

Farm Letters

Practice the letter **H** for horse. Have students color the giant letters on this page. Ask them if they can make the uppercase **H** look like a fence. Then have them draw a horse jumping over the fence. They can do this on the back of their papers, if desired.

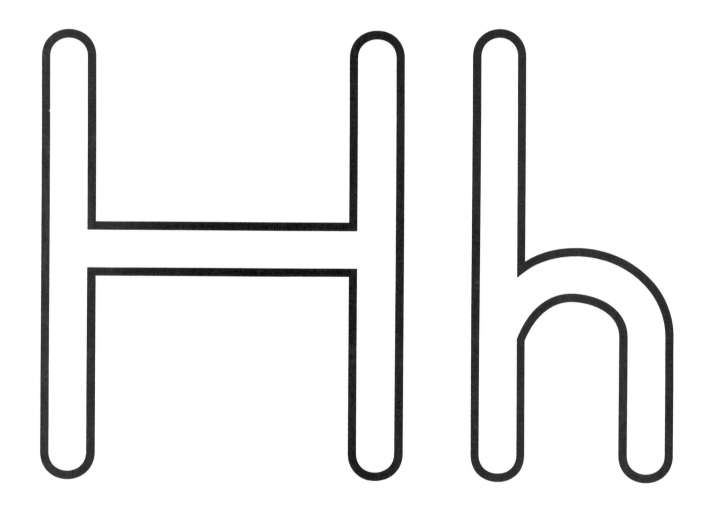

A reward badge for this activity can be found on page 79.

Farm Numbers

Duplicate the squares below onto heavy paper for students. Cut out the individual squares. Give each student several squares of each animal.

Choose a number and ask students to make a set of that quantity for a certain animal. For example, if you tell students to make a set of five ducks, they should count five ducks from their individual piles. You can make this activity more complex by asking students to gather sets of two or more different kinds of animals, each in either the same or different amounts. You can also practice making patterns and doing basic addition and subtraction facts with these squares.

Farm Music

Trace the patterns below onto felt and cut them out. Sing "Old MacDonald" (Holiday, 1989; North South, 1994) together, placing each pattern on the flannel board at the appropriate time. You may wish to keep the pieces in order on the flannel board so that students can remember the sequence while singing the song at another time.

A reward badge for this activity can be found on page 79.

Farm Music *(cont.)*

Farm Movement

Place copies of the clip art patterns (page 78) or the animal squares (page 70) in a hat. Let each student draw an animal from the hat and pantomime it for the class. Each student can make the animal's sound as well as its movements. Encourage students to guess the name of each animal that is pantomimed.

Farm Food

Ask parents to send a variety of foods that grow on a farm. Below is a note to parents and a sign-up sheet that you can use. Sample the foods during snack time.

Dear Parents,

We are learning about farms in our classroom. We would like to sample a variety of foods that are

grown on farms. Please help us by sending some_____ or _____
                                                                (food item)   (food item)

on _____.
          (date)

Thank you,

_____   ☐ Yes, I can send the food.

                                                  ☐ No, I cannot send the food.

                                                  ☐ Please note my child is allergic to _____ .

Sign-Up List

- apples _____

- carrots _____

- tomatoes _____

- lettuce _____

- radishes _____

- potatoes _____

- rice cereal _____

- wheat cereal _____

- corn cereal _____

- oat cereal _____

Animal Sounds

Can you make the sounds that each of these animals makes?

Old MacTavish

Yes, Old MacDonald had a farm—
The greatest place around.
But all that changed on one fine day
When MacTavish came to town.

MacTavish is a farming man,
The best there's ever been.
He has the most amazing farm—
Oh, where should I begin?

On his farm he has a horse,
But not the normal kind.
This horse is a magician,
The trickiest you can find.

And then he has a herd of cows
Who can play the fiddle,
While in the barn a flock of sheep
Dance right down the middle.

Then there are the chickens who—
Just to pass away the hours—
Gather all their speckled eggs
And build them into towers.

The pigs just seem like normal swine
But, strange as it appears,
They run the local grocery store—
The ducks are their cashiers.

At last, there are the billy goats,
Who, thinking they are sheep,
Lay their heads upon their pillows
And count themselves to sleep.

Yes, Old MacDonald had a farm,
But it could not compare
To Old MacTavish's barnyard
And the amazing animals there.

Clip Art and Patterns

Note: If you cut open the doors of the barn and glue the back of the rest of the barn onto white construction paper, students can draw some animals or glue the patterns from page 74 behind the barn doors.

Clip Art and Patterns *(cont.)*

Bookmarks and Badges

My
favorite farm
animal is the

_____ .

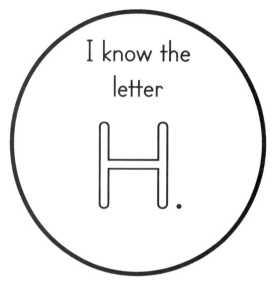

I know the
letter

H.

Write in each student's choice. Let
students color their badges and wear
them home.

Have students color their badges and
wear them home.

Farmer

_____

Let's read
about farms.

I know
what the
animals say.

MOO

OINK

Let each student write his or her name
on the line, color the badge, and wear it
while enjoying the foods from the farm
(page 73).

Although most early childhood students
have not yet learned to read, they enjoy
having bookmarks to use while reading
with their families at home.

Achievement Award

_____

has earned our

Classroom Achievement Award

for being a

Good Helper!

_____
Teacher's Signature

_____
Date